The Little Book of Anxiety

Chris Taylor

Illustrations by John Cooper

Foreword

Let me introduce myself; my name is Chris Taylor and I have been a counsellor for longer than I care to remember. Over that time I have become increasingly aware of the massive impact anxiety has on our lives. I've also realised with the best will in the world I can only ever help a small fraction of that number. So I began wondering how could I help more people, and it was those thoughts that are the origin of this book.

If you have ever doubted the existence of anxiety in ourselves and the society we live in, go shopping on Christmas Eve. Anxiety is that feeling of discomfort all around us. It manages to turn enjoyment into at best a chore, at worst complete burnout.

Franklin D. Roosevelt famously said, "the only thing we have to fear is fear itself ", and in many ways he was right. Of course, (unfortunately) it is a bit more complicated than that. Anxiety can be debilitating and at its worst downright frightening, and it has the ability to play tricks on all of us. There was not enough space in this book to deal with all the other conditions closely associated with anxiety; Intrusive Thoughts, Obsessive Compulsive Disorder, Free Floating Anxiety to name but three. Please forgive me, maybe next time!

However, I have included Panic Attacks; for the simple reason, I have rarely if ever worked with somebody experiencing anxiety who did not also experience panic attacks. So you could say panic, attacks, are included by popular demand. As for the rest of the book I hope my intentions are self-evident. I wanted to create a book that was easy for anyone to use and follow, no complicated theoretical debate, just solid practical help. Easy to follow particularly if you are feeling distressed at the time. Everything contained within this book, I have used in my work. So I know it works; all you have to do is decide what looks like the best fit for you. A word of warning; it's very tempting to charge straight ahead and go for possible solutions to your difficulties and ignore the importance of keeping safe. If you are not in a safe place when you start working on your anxiety it can very easily unravel and bite you on the bum so lets get safe first.

I will leave you now with two important thoughts, if you are feeling particularly anxious or worry and self doubt are starting to dominate your life. Please, please talk to somebody about how you're feeling. Secondly and this is a point easily forgotten, we all possess the power to change things for the better.

Introduction

Erma Bombeck described anxiety as a rocking chair, "it gives you something to do but it doesn't get you very far." If that sounds familiar then you probably need to read the rest of this book.

So why is anxiety such a big thing? That's a very good question, and one I hope to go some way towards answering. Of course, anxiety isn't new and it is definitely part of what it is to be human. In fact, my first tip is to recognise whether you are an anxious person or not.

By the way; if you're not an anxious person you can leave now.

Let's try not to think of anxiety like the enemy within, it is not some alien inhabiting our body, it is very much part of who and what we are. Anxiety is something we all share there is some of it in every single one of us. By acknowledging this about ourselves we are getting off to a very good start, believe me!

It's all too easy to think about anxiety as an entirely negative thing but it's not! It has its uses or we wouldn't have it in the first place. First and foremost, like fear it is there to protect us. Also like fear it can energise us into action and to do things we wouldn't normally do, solve problems and mobilise us to take the fight to where it needs to go.

That's the good stuff; what about the not so good stuff? One thing is for certain, worrying about worry never helped anybody. Second tip let's not worry about it, let's do something about it.

Here comes the government health warning, the dark stuff and why we all need to work with our own anxieties.

We all have anxieties, usually they developed from some incident in our past that we found either traumatic or in some way disturbing and for whatever reason was not dealt with at the time. However, if we don't recognise the event or possible series of events for what they are and do nothing about them, there is a very real possibility they can grow into something quite ugly and increasingly difficult to deal with.

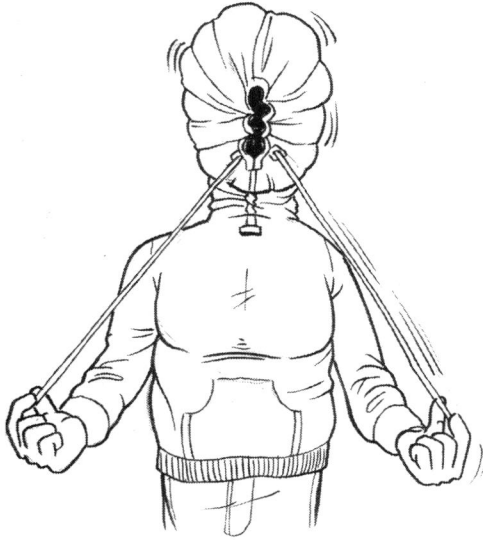

It's always worth remembering anxiety is an empire builder, if it sees any chink in our emotional armour it will quickly occupy its newfound territory, particularly if we don't recognise it for what it is.

Don't worry help is at hand.

So let's recap; what have we learnt so far? It's not a good idea to think about anxiety as a bad thing, it is very much part of who we are. The important thing is to recognise it and do something about it, if we think it's getting out of hand. Perhaps the most important thing is to remember You Are Not Alone. This is something that affects all of us, it's what we do about it that important.

What does Anxiety Look Like?

Anxiety can be tricky to identify especially in ourselves. Anger for example is often confused with anxiety and that is probably not surprising because in most cultures anxiety is more acceptable than expressions of anger. However, if you are feeling desperate, nervous, shocked, or threatened these are all emotions closely associated with fear and where there's fear there is usually anxiety.

Some physical things to look out for:

- rapid and/or irregular heartbeat
- fast breathing
- weakened or tense muscles
- sweating
- churning stomach or loose bowels
- dizziness
- dry mouth

Some psychological things to look out for:

- trouble sleeping
- lack of concentration
- feeling irritable
- feeling depressed
- loss of self-confidence

Please forgive me I will have to get a little bit technical here. The part of our brain responsible for learning and memory (the Amygdala) is also interestingly responsible for our behaviour and response to fear. Now you're not telling me there isn't some connection there!

The amygdala Is usually tightly controlled by the Prefrontal Cortex and it will decide if the information it is receiving is threatening or not. However, it appears if we have issues around anxiety, the brain can make an incorrect decision about what to fear and the amygdala will then put the whole body in fight, flight or freeze mode.

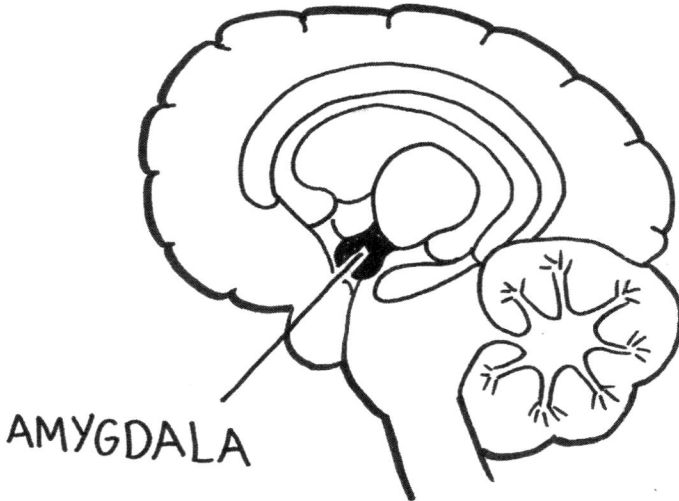

AMYGDALA

Now I suspect you're asking **why does it do that?**

As the politicians say; that's a very good question; the truth is we don't really know! One theory that makes some sense to me goes like this. The brain doesn't like gaps; if it hasn't got all the information it needs it will fill in the gaps, with what seems to fit but this might not be right because it didn't have all the information in the first place. It's rather like seeing something out of the corner of your eye and deciding what it is without turning to look at it properly and then decide.

The amygdala plays an important role in processing our emotions but it can also match identities, for example, facial recognition, sight, sounds and smells. This is known as a "Pattern Matching" if the amygdala recognises a situation that caused us distress in the past, it will automatically identify any similar situation in the future and this can be a source of anxiety. It seems all these functions are closely linked to our survival and keeping us safe. So if we encounter something that proved dangerous in the past, the amygdala reminds us of that danger even though everything else may now be different. So its warning maybe no longer necessary but we will still get the message and the emotional response.

One thing is for certain anxiety can and does affect our perception of the world around us. At the risk of getting a bit metaphysical, I think there is a very real possibility that if we could take in everything at the same time our brains would have simply be overwhelmed by information we could not process. So perhaps that is the true nature of anxiety is a focusing mechanism. By excluding and concentrating on certain information, it could be argued anxiety helps to keep us safe.

Panic Attacks

So what is a panic attack?

If you have ever experienced a sudden episode of intense fear and anxiety without any obvious reason, you have probably experienced a panic attack. One thing everybody agrees on is that they are terrifying, extremely frightening and physically and emotionally exhausting experiences.

Some physical things you might notice if you're having a panic attack:

- Rapid shallow breathing
- Your heart racing
- Tightness in the chest
- Trembling and shaking
- A choking feeling
- Sweating
- Feeling sick
- Blurred sight.

Some emotional things you might notice when having a panic attack.

- Fear of dying
- Feeling detached from your surroundings
- Confused and disoriented.

How long does a panic attack last?

The official figures go like this; a panic attack will peak within 10 minutes, then begin to subside. This period can last up to an hour but more usually somewhere between 20 to 30 minutes. Personally having worked a lot with people experiencing panic attacks, I suspect the come down period is much shorter, somewhere in the region of six minutes on average. Is also possible to have a series of panic attacks and this clearly makes it more difficult to work out any exact timings.

So why do I think that?

I think what people are feeling is the after effects of a panic attack, if you like the emotional and physical fallout. I know for anyone experiencing a panic attack it feels so much longer but I strongly suspect it's not.

I can hear you asking why?

For one simple and very straightforward reason, I believe the body cannot stand a sustained physical and emotional attack for anything up to an hour. I suspect the body recognises threat to our wellbeing and shuts the attack down relatively quickly.

So can you die from a panic attack?

The good news is, no one has ever died of a panic attack.

So what can we do?

I feel getting to know your panic attack and how it works is quite simply the best way to start.

A good question to ask yourself; is there any particular situation, person or event that happens before you have a panic attack? This is known as a **'trigger'**.

I don't think anything happens without a reason. Now this might be historical, something buried deep in our past, something we have forgotten or chosen to forget. Submerged memories like this can be triggered by sights, smells, sounds and even taste. Any one of our senses can trigger memories both good and bad

Panic attacks can also be triggered by phobias, particularly negative emotions and genetic factors can also play their part. If you are depressed or are bipolar for example, chances are you're more lightly to experience panic attacks.

So can we stop a panic attack?

I think the short answer is yes; if we know the origin of our panic attacks we are in a much better position to do something about them. That's why it's so important to work out what triggers the attack.

Next thing have a plan in place, so knowing what lies at the heart of your panic attack will be extremely helpful here. For example, you could know what situations, people, things to avoid or at least be cautious of.

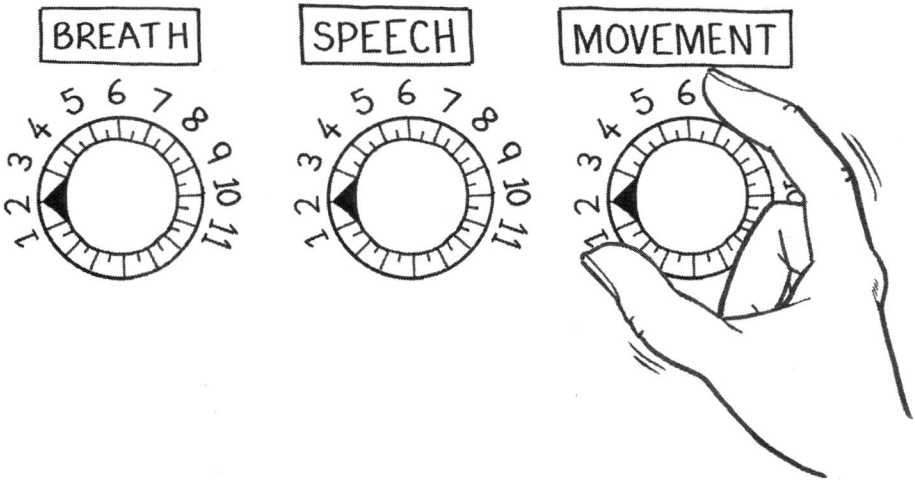

Slow everything down; remember our old friend the amygdala? Well slowing things down allows the frontal cortex time to examine what is going on and if it decides there is no threat it will shut the amygdala down, So you will not experience any fight, flight or freeze reactions.

One way of doing this is to practice deep breathing, this makes sense on two counts. Firstly you don't require any equipment and secondly one of the most common features of a panic attack is shallowness of breathing or "hyperventilating" if you prefer! By focusing on your breathing you refocus attention away from the attack and give you and your brain time to realise you are not under attack in any way.

Alternatively you could find an object to focus on, you could notice its colour, shape or even texture. This works in a very similar way by focusing your attention away from the attack and giving your brain time to realise there is no threat present .

In a similar way you could also try Visualisation, this technique engages with our creativity and I suspect that is why it can be so powerful and so effective. It also turns us into the objective observer, without judgement we can safely leave fear behind. Try and imagine yourself in some place where you were happy and felt entirely safe, for example on a beautiful beach somewhere, try to think of every detail of your surroundings and that moment in time.

Visualisation can be used in a variety of different ways, remember the last time you felt anxious and frightened, what did it feel like? Did it perhaps feel like something tightening into a knot in the pit of your stomach. If this sounds familiar visualisation can be very helpful. Start to turn the abstract fear into something concrete something you can work with by asking it series of questions:

- How big is it?
- How heavy is it?
- What does it look like?
- What colour is it?

Remarkably the abstract fear that was overwhelming you has become more manageable, even more understandable. By turning the abstract into the concrete we can start to control our fears rather than letting our fears control us.

To sum up; you know how to identify a panic attack, also it's not going to kill you. You have an idea of how to work with your panic attacks and some strategies that might help you keep on the right side of a panic attack. I think a panic attack is like falling off a cliff, the idea is to slow things down and stop you from falling over the edge.

Sleep

We tend not to think about sleep much; until we're not getting it, that itself is telling. We tend to think of sleep as one continuous process, it is in fact a cycle that lasts 90 minutes and during that time we move through five stages of sleep. The first four stages make up our non-rapid eye movement (NREM) sleep. You are more likely to have heard of the fifth stage known as (REM) sleep, rapid eye movement. It may help to think about our sleep like a graph going up and down in a continuous pattern rather than a one straight line.

REM sleep makes up 20 to 25% of average night sleep, it is also where we dream and where we regulate our memories and emotions. So I think it's fair to say that getting a good night's sleep is very important to us and why we become so vulnerable when we don't get enough sleep. We need to find a different time when you can worry about these things. Three in the morning is not a good time, because your body's metabolism is functioning at a very low level and nowhere near effective enough to deal with our concerns.

So we need to refocus and turn the negative into a positive, this can be done in a variety of different ways you just have to find the one that suits you best. Some people use familiar songs other people do mental arithmetic. Thinking about a story you have heard or a happy memory can also be very effective in changing our focus away from the worrying thoughts towards something altogether more positive comforting.

Having a regular routine before we go to bed can be extremely helpful, it simply prepares the brain for going to sleep and making sure your bedroom is a restful environment also helps enormously. Then in the morning we can plan for the future and when these plans can be best implemented.

Sleep journal

There is a lot of evidence to suggest we get emotional release from keeping a journal and it does help to lower our anxiety and achieve a better night's sleep. Choose a set time and place to write in your journal. It should be the same every day (e.g. in the bedroom room from 6:00 to 6:20 pm.) so it's early enough not to make you anxious right before bedtime. During this time you can worry about whatever is on your mind. The rest of the day can become a worry-free zone.

- What to write?
- Can you know how to fix the problem?
- Do you need to fix the problem or is it something that will take care of itself?
- Do you know what to do about the problem, or do you need to ask somebody else?
- Is the problem simply something completely out of your control?

If an anxious thought or worry comes into your head during the day, make a brief note of it on paper and postpone it to your worry period. Remind yourself that you'll have time to think about it later. So there's no need to worry about it now. Save it for later and carry on with your day.

During your journey time in the evening you can then reflect on the worries you wrote down during the day. If the thoughts are still bothering you allow yourself to worry about them, but only for the amount of time you've specified for your worry time. If the worries don't seem that important any more, cut down your worry time and enjoy the rest of your day.

So why does this work?

Personally I suspect it has a lot to do with our conditioning, we have had at least 6000 years of writing things down. We don't have to remember something if we've written it down and perhaps even more importantly there is the creative process of writing itself. In order to write something down we have to process it first, it has to make sense at least to us.

We have to make a lot of decisions in order to construct a sentence and while we're doing that, we're processing our thoughts.I suppose on one level it could even be described as a "Mindful" activity in that we are concentrating on one moment at the time. One word of warning; avoid using technology,it simply lacks the hold over us the handwritten word has. The reason? Quite possibly where we came in, with conditioning and that long history of writing things down.

Awareness

I think awareness is very good place to be. Awareness is when we realised something is not quite right and we are prepared to do something about it.

Chances are you will start to notice you are worrying about one particular thing or a group of related things. Hold that thought it's very important!

It's not my intention to simplify this too much but I think an example at this point would help. So for me it is missing a connecting flight and I suspect you can work this one out for selves.

Yes that's right!

Once upon a time; I missed my flight and even to this day somewhere at the back of my mind there is a nagging thought that I might miss my next flight.

Here's the rub; <u>negative thoughts have a habit of feeding on each other.</u> I begin with worrying about missing the next flight, can I get another flight and when, if not where will I stay and then how much will it cost?

See how it works, in no time at all I have made a mountain out of a molehill.

Here comes a really important point to remember, chances are none of this will happen. So why am I worrying about what Is probably not going to happen?

Well, I hate to break the bad news like this but our brains are not hard wired to make us happy (we have to do that for ourselves) our brains are wired up to help us survive. That is why our thoughts keep returning to negative emotions, past mistakes, and worries about the future.

I feel the need to defend our brains, their primary function is to keep us safe and In order to do this our brains default position is beware of that negative experience that happened. If we're worrying about "that bad thing" as far as our brains are concerned they are doing their job.

The fact that we all have worries I would say that is perfectly normal. The important point to remember is what we do about them. In short do we let them control us or do we control them, that's really the question we need to be asking ourselves.

So we now have some idea of how anxiety operates and why. Our anxiety usually stems from an incident or possibly a set of experiences. Negative thoughts will feed off each other and our brain's principal function is to keep us safe not to make us happy- that's our job.

History

Hopefully we have started to have at least some understanding over why we worry and maybe even what we are worrying about.

So why are we worrying? What is it doing for us?

A more accurate question maybe what did it do for us and why is it not working anymore?

Negative feelings and emotions such as shame, guilt and criticism may well help us to survive as young children but as we grow older our emotional needs change and develop. Survival strategies that worked when we were young no longer work in our adult lives.

The difficulties come when we reach adulthood and continue to follow the same script and don't notice the rules have changed and we have changed.

We have many more options now and our emotional needs are very different. As a child we need to survive, as an adult we have very different emotional needs for example relationships, a sense of purpose and achievement. In many ways we need these things to validate who and what we are as adults. If we are to achieve these things, we also need to allow for continued growth and the degree of vulnerability.

As children we are fearful for our own survival and (quite rightly so) so we endeavour to please and not offend, for fear of reprisals and of course, it must be remembered we are usually unaware that our upbringing is any different from anybody else's.

After saying all that it's also worth remembering that anxiety can also creep up on us in later life. Usually associated with a specific event, that anxiety exploits all too quickly.

To briefly recap negative emotions from childhood have a lasting effect and we can all too easily carry them into adulthood were they don't fit with the life we want to lead. If fear and anxiety continue to control us we cannot become the person we want to be. That's why our emotional history is so important to understanding anxiety.

Staying Safe

What do I mean by staying safe?

Before we start the difficult job of unpicking what lies at the bottom of our anxieties, it is good to put in place something that will help to support us through that often and let's be honest here quite difficult process of realising what lies at the bottom of our fears and anxiety.

Distraction: this needs to be a short term strategy (but necessary) to take care of yourself. Do something that makes you feel better and help you relax, for example, watching television, going out for a walk or even doing the ironing.

Routine: it's easy to overlook the importance of structure in our daily lives, after are all creatures of habit. We like ritual and predictability, don't forget it's unpredictability and not knowing that makes us anxious. It helps in other ways as well you can easily keep track of what you've done and the monitoring achievements is valuable. It can also prevent self-destructive impulses and by having a routine before we go to bed we are much more likely to experience a good night's sleep.

Compassion

Appreciation: focusing on an activity you enjoy or have enjoyed in the past. You could for example make a list of things you like, things that give us pleasure. It can be a treasured memory from our past. Just try reliving that moment and it's amazing how quickly it can create that much needed moment of calm and space.

Practice gratitude: be grateful for who you are, your friends and family or what you have achieved. I know this can sound a bit like we patting ourselves on the back but the important point is we are concentrating on the good stuff not the bad.

Reconnect: with people we love, what we enjoyed about our job or an interest we once had, be creative.

Mindfulness: the idea of meditation in my experience does not appeal to everybody. I think it is important to remember how it can help us in very practical ways and it really is very simple. All this involves is paying attention to the current moment in a non-judgemental way. Simply accepted it for what it is and use your strongest sense. So for example it is auditory, concentrate on the ticking of a clock. Another very popular misconception about meditation is that it is passive. This couldn't be further from the truth, you are very purposefully concentrating on the ticking of the clock. That is the very point. Your concentration excludes everything else that is going on around you.

Reflection: this is simply taking 20 minutes out of your day to think about what we have done how it has affected you and what does it feel like? Early evening is a good time to do this, so what you are not still thinking about it when you go to bed.

Triggers

Start to try and recognise those triggers we talked about earlier what are they, where they came from and how do they affect you?

They can be virtually anything, depending on our experiences but losing control, relationships, finances, confrontation, meeting new people, health, comparisons and performance are just some examples you might recognise.

Depending on what we identify our triggers to be, it could be a good idea at this stage to start looking at control what means for you and do we need to have it, if so why? This same approach can be applied to any of the other possible triggers I have mentioned or of course, something particular to yourself.

This is also a good place to start a journal, looking at how anxiety affects you, what do you think your triggers might be, why you think that is and what could you possibly do about it?

To sum up; in order to keep ourselves safe we need to start thinking positively about situations no matter how bleak they might appear to be. What often gets forgotten is the importance of evaluating the effects these soothing strategies can and do have on us, so don't forget to make a note of you feel.

Avoidance

By avoiding a situation that
makes us anxious we are simply
reinforcing our negative beliefs
about the situation. By avoiding
the situation we are giving anxiety
space to grow and at the same
time eroding our self-confidence.
We may think we are doing the
best thing for ourselves but in
reality we often end up beating ourselves up with more
negative self-talk and that in turn results in feeling more
intimidated the next time.

What all too often gets forgotten here is the importance of
being kind to ourselves reward yourself for what you have
achieved and in that way you can stop negative thoughts in
their tracks. If you are having a bad day try not to worry about
it and remember just because something bad happened one
day does not mean it will happen the next day.

Avoidance just doesn't work we are only making it more
difficult for ourselves, storing up trouble for next time. We
have to face our fears and become more comfortable with the
uncomfortable.

How do I do this?

There are several things you can do to prepare for a situation you were going to find difficult to deal with:

You can change the way you think about the situation from negative to positive. I can do rather than I cannot do. It's often the story we tell ourselves that is more frightening

Remember you have more power than you may think you have, you do not have to say yes something you do not agree with.

Be particularly aware of comparing yourself to others, we are not the same and never will be. We are different from each other, we look at things differently, have different experiences and we do things differently. The important point to remember there is nothing wrong with difference quite the reverse embrace your individuality

We also need to recognise that each and every one of us has prejudices and prejudices can get in the way if we let them so be aware of yours. These can be anything from politicians to be certain colour, the point is no matter how small they may be they can get in the way of us doing what we need to do

Finally allow yourself some time each day to reflect on your feelings and how you reacted to them. Even better to write then down.

So the next time we are in that difficult situation that one which frightens us so much. We have done all the groundwork, it's time to face the music! If you feel your anxiety rising rather than abandon the situation try taking three deep breaths and keep in there.

Chances are before you know it you will have beaten your anxiety, just remember to keep doing it every time you feel nervous. It's also worth remembering avoidance can take on many forms, rumination and procrastination, are just two of its many forms to beware of.

Recognising rumination and procrastination

Anyone who ruminates will tend to think repeatedly about their negative emotional experiences. Procrastination is slightly different; rather than continuously thinking about the same thing you will avoid certain situations or tasks that feel unsure about. I suppose the big differences is procrastination is something most of us have done at some time in our lives.

Working With Anxiety

Before we go any further, here is the Government Health Warning, if you are an anxious person you will always be an anxious person.

Don't get too depressed, or else I will have to write another book, it's not as bad as it sounds.

It's just that I think it's all too easy to see anxiety as the enemy within. But it's not, it is just part of who and what we are as human beings and it's certainly not my intention to change who you are. What I hope to do this book is, help you live more comfortably with this part of your personality.

Things do start to get better once we realise worrying is the problem not the solution.

Fear only allow us to see the down side of things and fear all too easily leads to anxiety and to the dark side. It also obstructs our natural intuition, stopping us going with our first thought or just how we feel about something, our gut reaction.

You may find it hard to give up your worries because they have become part of you. Worrying is undoubtedly addictive and habit forming that's the trap, it offers us security in an uncertain world where we can't take anything for granted.

This is where I think worry is both at its most beguiling and dangerous. Worry will tell you it's working for you not against you and by worrying It will help you:

- Find a solution
- Stop you overlook anything
- If I keep thinking a bit longer, I will figure it out
- There won't be any nasty surprises
- It would be irresponsible of me not to worry about it
- It's too important not to worry about
- If I worry about it it'll be ok.

Or your worry could be that you're going to lose all control over your worrying, it will take over and never stop.

Recognising what we can and what we can't control is very important, because it's only when we start noticing this in ourselves that we can ask the question, if we can't change it, why are we worried about it?

However, at this stage we are all a bit like the proverbial three legged stool, take a leg away and we will fall over, so we need to our focus on keeping safe.

Let's take a moment; there is some important stuff here. Recognising you are an anxious person and this is not necessarily a bad thing. Anxiety is not the enemy within. The danger is it only allows us to focus on the downside of things. We also looked at why we hang on to our worries, Not forgetting at this stage we are still vulnerable so it is important to remain focused on staying safe.

Strategies

All the following strategies I have personally used in my work as a counsellor, unfortunately what I cannot do here is suggest which one might be best for you. Perhaps the best way forward is to see which one you like the look of and try it, see if it works for you. If it doesn't try another one and if that doesn't work I would suggest you seek further help. Whatever you eventually decide please please do not suffer in silence.

Apologies if that's all a bit heavy but the aim of this book is to help you through this difficult part of your life, so onwards and upwards!

Worry time

Create a "worry time" Choose a set time and place for worrying. It should be the same every day (e.g. in the bedroom room from 6:00 to 6:20 pm.) so it's early enough not to make you anxious right before bedtime.

During your worry period you can worry about whatever is on your mind. The rest of the day however, is a worry-free zone.

Postpone your worry" If an anxious thought or worry comes into your head during the day, make a brief note of it on paper and postpone it to your worry period. Remind yourself that you'll have time to think about it later. So there's no need to worry about it now. Save it for later and carry on with your day.

Go over your "worry list" during the worry period. Reflect on the worries you wrote down during the day. If the thoughts are still bothering you allow yourself to worry about them, but only for the amount of time you've specified for your worry time. If the worries don't seem that important any more, cut down your worry time and enjoy the rest of your day.
I can hear you asking how is that going to help?

Give me a moment and I will explain.

Postponing worrying is effective because it breaks the habit of dwelling on worries in the present moment. Yet there's no struggle to suppress the thoughts or judge them. We simply save them for later. As you develop the ability to postpone your anxious thoughts you will start to realise that you have more control over your worrying than you thought.

Leading us neatly onto the next strategy.

This is intended to be a more flexible approach towards tackling worry and anxiety. It draws on different strands of thought regarding how anxiety can best be tackled. You could decide to use just one of these techniques or all three, alternatively use them in combination with the other two strategies I have included here.

The objective observer

To me as a counsellor this strategy always seems a little counterintuitive; we spend so much time encouraging people to get in touch with her feelings and here I am trying to get you to disassociate yourself from them. But as one client one said to me "it is what it is" and that about sums it up!
I think the best way to think about this strategy is to think of yourself as the counsellor looking at your concerns objectively and without judgement. Think about how much easier it is to deal with other people's problems than it is to deal with our own.

If we create a bit of distance between ourselves and our feelings, things can look very different. Once we start to look at our worries objectively it is amazing how quickly we can see them for what they are. We can then start questioning do we really need them, why am I holding on to them and what are they doing to me?

It was once described to me as standing on a river bank and watching the river flow past. If you can create some distance between your anxieties and how you feel about them you will be in a much stronger position to deal with them.

Be the observer — without judgment.

Practice observing your (thoughts, feelings, emotions and sensations) with compassion.

RELATIONSHIPS

WORK   MONEY   FAMILY

Worry mountain

Make your way down from the top and decide which route best describes your particular issue. Continue following your chosen route down the mountain until you get to "what, where and how" and decide whether you need to deal with this issue now or later.

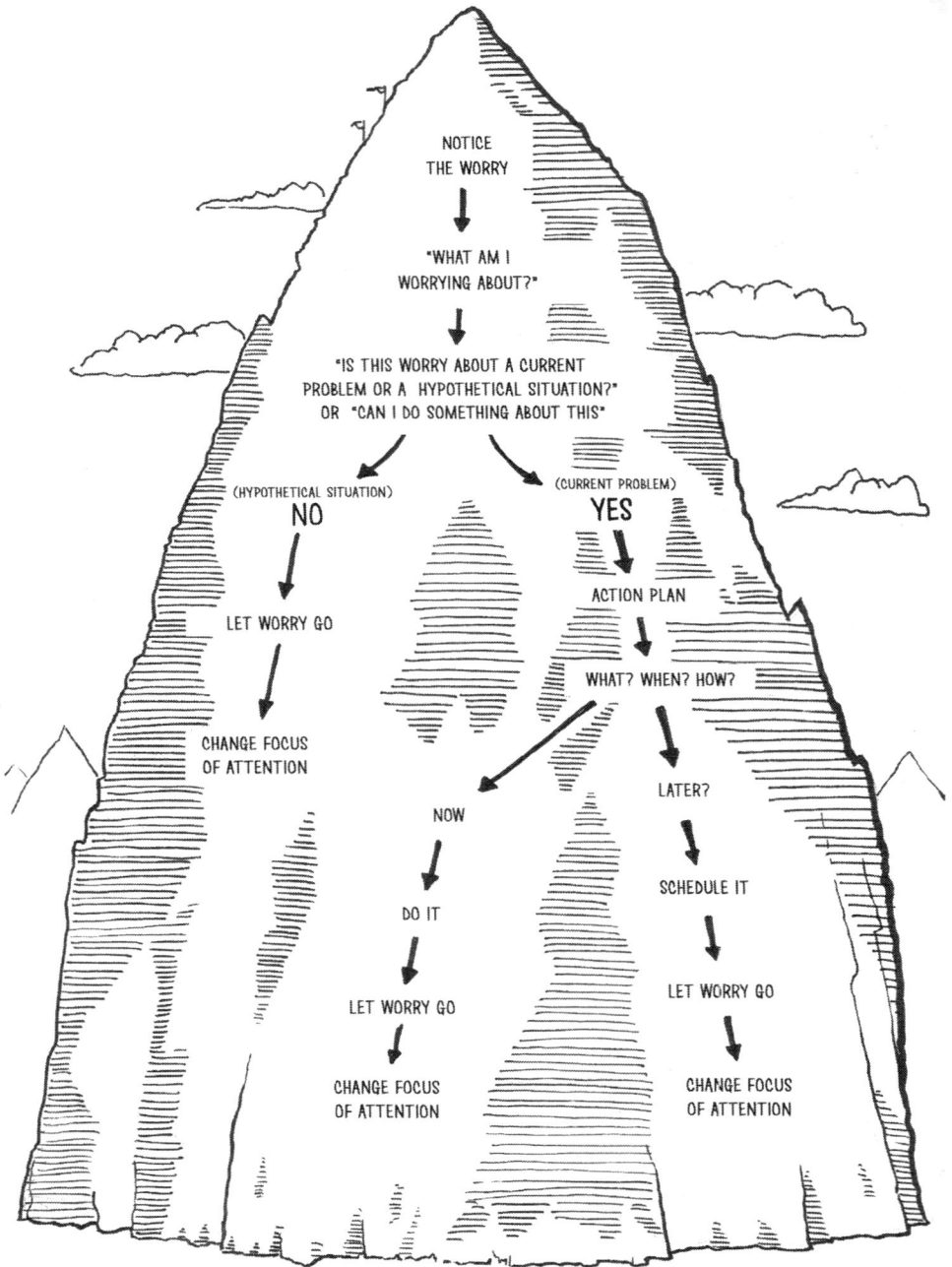

NOTICE
THE WORRY
↓
"WHAT AM I
WORRYING ABOUT?"
↓
"IS THIS WORRY ABOUT A CURRENT
PROBLEM OR A HYPOTHETICAL SITUATION?"
OR "CAN I DO SOMETHING ABOUT THIS"

(HYPOTHETICAL SITUATION)
NO

(CURRENT PROBLEM)
YES
↓
ACTION PLAN
↓
WHAT? WHEN? HOW?

LET WORRY GO
↓
CHANGE FOCUS
OF ATTENTION

NOW
↓
DO IT
↓
LET WORRY GO
↓
CHANGE FOCUS
OF ATTENTION

LATER?
↓
SCHEDULE IT
↓
LET WORRY GO
↓
CHANGE FOCUS
OF ATTENTION

Decluttering

Looking at your worries objectively allows you to decide what
is worth keeping and what you can get rid of. Throughout our
lives we accumulate thoughts, experiences and we develop ways
of reacting to these thoughts and experiences, some are good
some are not so good. What we have to do; is decide what to
keep and what to get rid of, what is of no use to us anymore and
maybe even getting in the way of what we do want.

Let me suggest you get a packet of "post it" notes clear the
kitchen table and create two columns "things I no longer need"
and "things I do need." Then write on the post it notes every
thought, feeling that pops into your head. Then put them in
the appropriate column and throw away the ones you don't
need anymore. Be careful to keep any you are undecided about
until you are sure what you want to do with them.

You will probably be surprised by how much lighter you feel after completing this exercise.

This also works well with the physical things we all accumulate and we don't need anymore. I would suggest practicing the two year rule (unless it's something very special to you) if you haven't used it in that time you don't need it. This can be extremely cathartic to clear out all that old stuff we don't need anymore, it can give you a tremendous lift and feeling a freedom.

Plan ahead

Undoubtedly one of the greatest causes of anxiety is fear of the unknown and in many ways this fear makes perfect sense. What we don't know can of course, at the very least unsettling if not downright frightening.

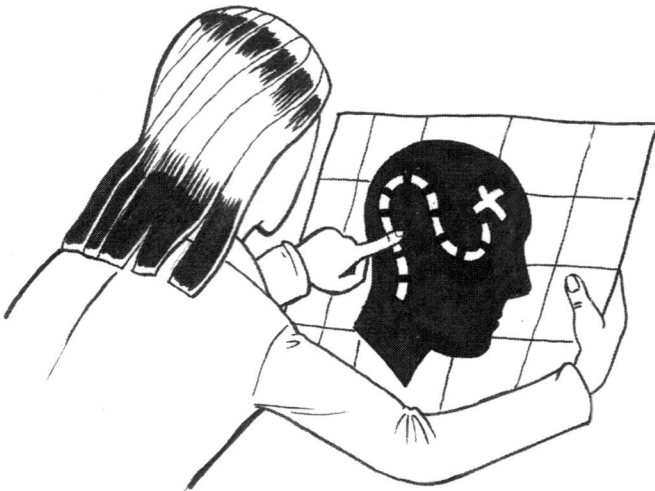

So what can we do?

I would suggest let's start to break it down into manageable chunks. I think everything will have to deal with can be broken down into at least three basic components.

Past, Present and Future

How does that help, I can hear you say!

Well to start with; once we break something down it's easier to deal with, we can tackle one part at a time. The past; we all carry a lot of emotional baggage around with us that we no longer need and if we go back to decluttering:
Yes you've got it!

We can get rid of a lot of stuff we no longer need, there will of course, be stuff we want to keep. Treasured memories, important experiences and learning. But there will be a lot of stuff we genuinely don't need any more. So this is your chance to get rid and I promise you will feel much better for it.

Now let's come to a very important point. We can't change the past. So what about the present? We can't change that either. All we can ever do is react and interact with whatever is going on around us that moment in time.

What about where our fears actually lives.

Yes you're right in the future.

Well even here we have more power than we often give ourselves credit for. We have a lot of learning experience, in many ways we have a good idea how things will turn out depending on how we choose to deal with them and we can plan accordingly. Think of it like a business plan for your life.

It's a good idea to keep the plan flexible and evaluate how it's working out and amended it accordingly. We can also have more than one plan in order to achieve the same objectives.

By dividing our fears and anxiety into past present and future we can almost automatically reduce our fear by two thirds. Fear does not live in the past or present but in the future and of course, we can never entirely predict what will happen in the future but we can plan for it. Then if that plan need some adjustment we can do that as well.

Planning for the future

Work through this sheet stage by stage, I feel this exercise recognises that bad things do happen but places the emphasis on what we can do about them. When you reach "How will I deal with these difficulties" it can be helpful to think about having more than one plan to reach the same ~~your~~ goal. It is also worth taking time ~~to~~ evaluating what you have achieved so far and remember there's always another way.

Distinguishing between solvable and unsolvable worries.

What is true and what is false?

If a worry pops into your our head we can start by asking ourselves whether this is an issue or something you can actually do something about?

The following questions can help us decide:

The problem something we are currently having to deal with? Or are we what-if-ing?

If the problem is a what-if, how likely is it to happen? So are our concerns realistic?

Can we do something about the problem or possibly prepare for it?

Or is it out of our control?

WHAT HAVE I LEARNED?

HOW CAN I BUILD ON THIS?   WHAT IS MY PLAN OF ACTION?

WHAT MIGHT MAKE IT DIFFICULT FOR ME TO PUT THIS PLAN INTO ACTION?

WHAT MIGHT MAKE IT DIFFICULT FOR ME TO PUT THIS PLAN INTO OPERATION?

HOW WILL I DEAL WITH THESE DIFFICULTIES?

WHAT MIGHT LEAD TO A SET BACK? (EG. LIFE STRESSES, PROBLEMS, RELATIONSHIPS)

IF I DO HAVE A SETBACK, WHAT WILL I DO ABOUT IT?

The three concentric circles

I think this diagram shows very clearly what we do and do not have control of in our lives. Also I feel if we concentrate our efforts in the second circle, this is where our own personal growth and development lies.

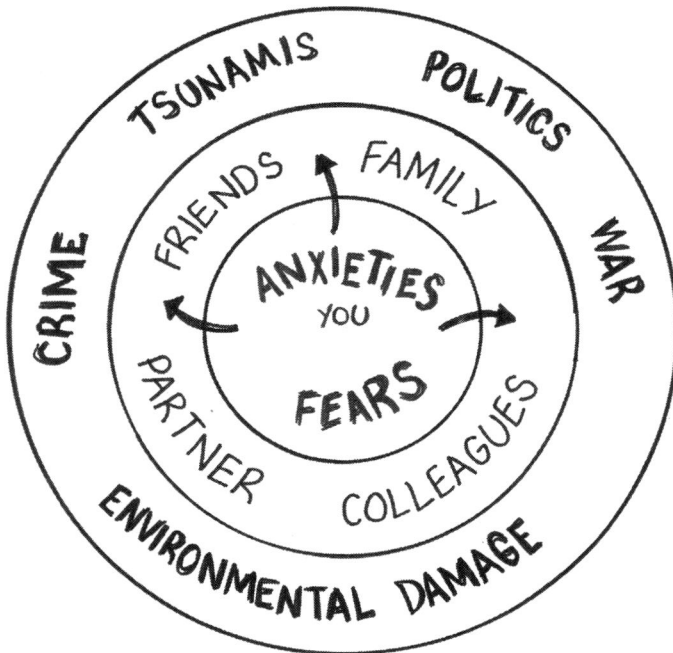

This is about recognising the difference between what we can control and what we can't. Solvable worries (as the name suggests) are those we can do something about and even take action straight away if necessary. If we were worried about not paying our bills on time we could call the creditors and arrange a more flexible payment option.

However, an unsolvable worry looks very different, these are worries where we can't do anything about them simply because either it hasn't happened yet or in all probability it won't ever happen. For example "what if" my plane crashes, "what if" I die of a heart attack or "what if" is my husband is killed driving home from work?

I suspect it is their very unsolvability that makes them so seductive, they never can be solved, so you will always have something to worry about.

Can you see it is a trap, the question we need to be asking ourselves why am I hanging on to this worry and what is it doing for me?

If the worry is solvable; start make a list of all the possible solutions you can think of. Try not to get too concerned about finding the perfect solution. Instead focus on the things you have the power to change, rather things beyond your control, like what's happening in the news. After you've looked at your options, make a plan of action. Once you have a plan you can start doing something about the problem.

Interrogating your anxiety

Sometimes it is helpful to dissect our anxiety in greater detail by asking the following questions:

- What is the evidence that this thought is true ?
- What is the evidence that this thought is not true?
- Is there a more positive realistic way of looking at this situation?
- What is the probability that what I am scared of will actually happen?
- If it is unlikely to happen, what is more likely to happen?
- Is the thought helpful?
- How will worrying about it help me and how could it hurt me?
- What would I say to a friend who have this worry?

One thing is certain anxiety does not like to be questioned, because once we start questioning our anxieties they start to lose their validity. Once we put anxiety under the spotlight it starts to wither and die and consequently lose its hold on us.

Conclusion

Anxiety; like many aspects of the brain's activities is still not yet fully understood. However, it does have some very recognisable characteristics and is clearly fundamental to the way we think. It certainly has the ability to make us focus on one particular thing, often to the exclusion of everything else. It also finds validity for its actions from our previous experiences. When we revisit these (often negative) experiences it only serves to reinforce our anxiety's hold over us. It's almost like that old parental phrase " I told you so."

Warning controversial bit coming up!

In all my years of working with anxiety I have noticed one another recurring theme. Though anxiety is usually what brings clients to counselling it is all too often the symptom not the disease (metaphorically speaking). Anxiety seems to act rather like an addiction, it appears to mask what is really going on. So understanding what lies beneath our anxiety is every bit as important as dealing with anxiety at self.

Let me leave you with one final thought. Nothing diminishes anxiety faster than action and the best action you can take is to talk to somebody you can trust about how you are feeling.

I would like to think by the time we have finished you will be no longer looking down at your shoes but up towards your Future.

Biography

Chris Taylor qualified as a counsellor in 2014 and is both BACP and NHS accredited, with his own private practice specialising in couples work and supervision. He has also worked for the last five years at Walthew House, counselling the visual impaired.
Prior to becoming a counsellor he works for a large local authority's social service's department for over 21 years, specialising in adults with learning difficulties.

Website: www.taylorcounselling.co.uk

Walthew House

Counselling Service

This is a non-profit making venture and any profits made will go to Walthew House (112 Shaw Heath, Stockport SK2 6QS. Reg charity number 1167749) an independent local charity supporting people in Stockport, who are blind, visually impaired, Deaf or hard of hearing.

Website: www.walthewhouse.org.uk

Printed in Poland
by Amazon Fulfillment
Poland Sp. z o.o., Wrocław